PRAYERS FOR EVERYONE

FRANK COLQUHOUN is a former Canon Residentiary and Vice-Dean of Norwich Cathedral. Previously, most of his life was spent in South London, where he was for seven years Vicar of Wallington and later Canon and Chancellor of Southwark Cathedral and Principal of the Southwark Ordination Course. Now retired, he lives at Bexhill in Sussex.

His many books include *Parish Prayers, Contemporary Parish Prayers and New Parish Prayers*. He is also editor of the revised edition of the BBC service book, *New Every Morning*. His previous books for triangle include *Family Prayers, Prayers for Today,* and *My God and King.*

Other Triangle Books by
Frank Colquhoun

FAMILY PRAYERS
PRAYERS FOR TODAY
MY GOD AND KING

Prayers for Everyone

compiled and edited by

FRANK COLQUHOUN

TRIANGLE

First published 1991
Triangle
SPCK
Holy Trinity Church
Marylebone Road
London NW1 4DU

Fourth impression 1996

British Library Cataloguing in Publication Data

A catalogue record for this book is available
from the British Library.

ISBN 0–281–04563–1

Typeset by Inforum Typesetting, Portsmouth
Printed in Great Britain by
BPC Paperbacks Ltd
A member of
The British Printing Company Ltd

Contents

Preface

The title of this further collection of prayers for Triangle Books provides the key to its contents.

Prayers intended for everyone must necessarily have a wide appeal and meet a variety of needs.

Accordingly the prayers I have chosen are of a very mixed character, covering a considerable number of topics and drawn from many sources, old and new.

Obviously not all the prayers will be of interest to everyone; but I hope that everyone will find among them something of help in the life of prayer.

The book is divided into clearly marked sections to enable the reader to find his way about. To facilitate reference an index of principal subjects is also included.

Frank Colquhoun

Note

An asterisk (*) added to the ascription of a prayer indicates that it has been slightly altered or shortened. Prayers described as 'Adapted' are derived from various sources, known and unknown, and have been considerably modified and rewritten by the Editor.

PART ONE

Lift Up Your Hearts

PRAISE THE LORD

Adoration of the Trinity 1

Worthy of praise from every mouth, of worship from every creature, is thy glorious name, O Father, Son, and Holy Spirit, who didst create the world by the word of thy power, and in love didst wonderfully redeem it.

Wherefore with angels and archangels, and all the company of heaven, we adore and magnify thy name, evermore praising thee and saying:

Holy, Holy, Holy, Lord God of hosts,
Heaven and earth are full of thy glory:
Glory be to thee, O Lord most high.

Nestorian Liturgy (6th century)

2

Blessing and honour, thanksgiving and praise,
   more than we can utter,
   more than we can conceive,
be unto thee, O holy and glorious Trinity,
   Father, Son, and Holy Spirit,
by all creatures, all men, all angels,
   for ever and ever.

Lancelot Andrewes (1555–1626)

O thou in whom all things live,
who commandest us to seek thee,
and art ever ready to be found:
  to know thee is life,
  to serve thee is freedom,
  to praise thee is our souls' delight.
We bless thee and adore thee,
we worship thee and magnify thee,
we give thanks to thee for thy great glory,
  through Jesus Christ our Lord.

St Augustine (354–420)

4

Almighty God, whose glory the heavens are telling, the earth thy power, the sea thy might, and whose greatness all feeling and thinking creatures everywhere proclaim: to thee belongeth glory, honour, might and magnificence, now and for ever, unto the ages of ages; through Jesus Christ our Lord.

Liturgy of St James (4th century)

5

Great, O Lord, is thy kingdom, thy power and thy glory; great also is thy wisdom, thy goodness, thy justice, thy mercy; and for all these we bless thee, and will magnify thy name for ever and ever.

George Wither (17th century)

To God the Father, who first loved us, and made us
  accepted in the Beloved;
to God the Son, who loved us, and washed us from
  our sins in his own blood;
to God the Holy Ghost, who sheds the love of God
  abroad in our hearts:
to the one true God be all love and all glory,
  for time and for eternity.

Thomas Ken (1637–1711)

THANKS BE TO GOD

God's many gifts 7

God of love, we give you thanks for the boundless
mercies of our daily life. Make us more grateful for
your many gifts:
  for the blessing of health,
  for the comforts of home and family life,
  for the joys of friendship,
  for the beauty of the world around us.
Teach us day by day to count our blessings and to
receive them as from our Father's hand; and fill our
hearts with gratitude and our lips with praise, for the
sake of Jesus Christ our Lord.

F.C.

Almighty God, more generous than any father, we
stand amazed at the many gifts you shower upon us.

You give freely and willingly, always with regard to
our ability to receive.

You give daily gifts, teaching us to trust you for
tomorrow.

You give us gifts through one another, so that we
may learn to share.

You give through our own effort, respecting our
independence.

How thoughtfully you offer all your gifts!

So continue, Lord, of your goodness.

Anon

9

We thank you, Lord, for all your goodness to us:

for the world you have made and for strength to
serve you in it;

for daily revelations of yourself in nature, in art, and
in the lives of men;

for the Bible through which you speak your word to
us;

for all other books which open our minds to your
truth;

for the tasks to which you are calling us.

May your Spirit dwell richly within us, enabling us to
serve you with gladness all the days our life;

through Jesus Christ our Lord.

*The Splendour of God**

Eternal God, we thank you for all you have given us, for all you have done for us, for all you are to us in your beloved Son.

    In our weakness you are strength,
    in our darkness you are light,
    in our sorrow you are comfort.

For all your mercies, we bless you, our Father,
May we live as ever in your presence and glorify you in our daily lives, for our Saviour's sake.

After St Boniface (8th century)

11

Glory be to God in the highest, the Creator and Lord of heaven and earth, the Father of mercies, who so loved mankind as to send his only Son into the world, to redeem us from sin and misery, and to obtain for us everlasting life. Accept, O God, our praise and thanksgiving for your infinite mercies towards us; and teach us to love you more and serve you better, for our Lord Jesus Christ's sake.

Bishop Gavin Hamilton (17th century)

GRATITUDE

Thanksliving 12

'Thanksgiving is good; thanksliving is better.'
Bishop J. Taylor Smith

Lord, write this truth on all our hearts, that thankful
for all your goodness and mercy,
we may show forth your praise, not only with our
lips but in our lives, by giving up ourselves to your
service, and by walking before you in holiness and
righteousness all our days.

Based on the General Thanksgiving,
Book of Common Prayer

Counting our blessings 13

God our Father, we would thank you for all the bright
things of life. Help us to see them, and to count them,
and to remember them, that our lives may flow in
ceaseless praise; through Jesus Christ our Lord.

J.H. Jowett (1864–1923)

Thou who hast given so much to me,
Give one thing more, a grateful heart . . .
Not thankful, when it pleases me;
As if thy blessings had spare days;
But such a heart whose very pulse may be
Thy praise.

George Herbert (1593–1633)

LORD, TEACH US TO PRAY

What is prayer? 15

Prayer is the soul's sincere desire,
 Uttered or unexpressed;
The motion of a hidden fire
 That trembles in the breast.

Prayer is the Christian's vital breath,
 The Christian's native air,
His watchword at the gate of death;
 He enters heaven by prayer.

James Montgomery (1711–1854)

> *At the moment Jesus died on the cross, the curtain of the temple was torn asunder from top to bottom, as by the hand of God, signifying that the way into his holy presence was now wide open to all.*

Our Father, we thank you for that open way, open still and open to all, open for evermore, through the sacrifice of your Son.

You are no longer hidden or separated from us but always accessible, always within reach of our prayers.

Therefore, as we are bidden, we come with confidence to your throne of grace, to obtain mercy and find your help in every time of need.

F.C.

The mystery of prayer 17

Lord God, prayer is a mystery. We don't understand how it works or how our feeble petitions reach heaven.

But we do know that Jesus prayed, and taught his disciples to pray, and that he opened the way into your presence.

Help us to follow his example and teaching, and learn to pray more naturally, more readily and more often, and always in his name.

*Llewellyn Cumings**

The one to whom we pray 18

Almighty God, you are always more ready to hear than we to pray, and to give more than either we desire or deserve: pour upon us the abundance of your mercy, giving us those good things which we are not worthy to ask, but through the merits and mediation of Jesus Christ our Lord.

Book of Common Prayer*

The spirit of prayer 19

Give us grace, Almighty Father, to address you with all our hearts as well as with our lips.

Teach us to fix our thoughts on you, reverently and with love, so that our prayers are not in vain, but are acceptable to you, now and always; through our Lord Jesus Christ.

Jane Austen (1775–1817)

PART TWO

Ourselves

WE ARE ALIVE

Man alive 20

Thank you, Lord, for the experience of being alive: for being able to feel, to think, to choose and to love.

Thank you for the delights and opportunities which each day brings.

Thank you for everything that makes life worth living, both for ourselves and for the sake of others.

Adapted from Richard Harries

God's gift 21

Lord of creation, the life we possess is your gift: we hold it in trust from you.

Teach us to value it and to use it wisely and responsibly, for we have but one life to live; one life in which to serve your Church, to advance your kingdom, and to be of help to others.

Show us your purpose for our life, and may we not live to be useless.

F.C.

Lord God Almighty, our Creator, as we bow in your presence we celebrate our existence, we rejoice in being alive.

Teach us to understand more and more profoundly that every human life is sacred, that each individual has been made in your image, and has been redeemed in Christ our Lord.

We ask this in his name.

From a prayer of Cardinal Basil Hume

Individuals 23

Heavenly Father, in the rush and hurry and busyness of life, help us to remember that each of us is not just one in a crowd, a mere nobody.

Far from that, each one is an individual, with our own personalities and responsibilities, our own life to live.

Above all, help us to remember that each of us is personally known to you, matters to you, is of worth to you, and that you love us each one.

F.C.

O God, teach us to know both our smallness and our greatness, our insignificance and our eternal worth.

Free us from all false pride, for we have nothing in ourselves of which to boast.

Help us rather to live each day with a sense of our true value: our value in your eyes, our maker and redeemer.

Adapted from Richard Harries

WE ARE PEOPLE

Contentment 25

Our Father, we pray for a more contented outlook on life.

Save us from a complaining spirit and from all envy and jealousy of the good of others.

Teach us to rejoice in what they have and we have not, to delight in what they can and we cannot achieve; and fill us daily with a sense of your love and of all your mercies to us; for our Saviour Jesus Christ's sake.

Adapted from W.A. Knight

Cheerfulness 26

Lord, give us at all times a cheerful spirit and a joyful sense of our blessings. Help us to look on the bright side of life, and save us from despondency and dejection, especially when the going is hard.

Increase our faith in your boundless and unchangeable love, and help us to remember at all times that the joy of the Lord is our strength.

F.C.

Courage 27

Lord Christ, you said to many people at various times,
'Be of good courage!'
  Speak that word to our hearts again and again, for
we all need courage:
    courage to hold fast to our Christian faith;
    courage to maintain a brave witness in the world;
    courage to overcome our fears and temptations;
    courage to persevere to the end of life's battle.
  Lord, in all these things give us good courage, and
make us more than conquerors through your love.

F.C.

Our speech 28

We thank you, Lord, for the power of speech. But let
us never forget that it is a power for evil as well as for
good.
  An ill-spoken word may cause irreparable hurt and
harm; a kindly word in season may bring immeasur-
able comfort and hope.
  So let us remember, especially before we speak too
hastily, that Jesus said: 'By your words you shall be
justified, and by your words you shall be condemned.'

F.C.

Our thinking 29

Deliver us, O God, from shallowness in our thinking and from following the superficial fashions of the world.

Save us from the worship of science and of earthly power and glory; that acknowledging our human reason as your precious gift, we may be freed from all false notions and misplaced trust, and put you first in our thinking, our God, and our salvation.

Adapted

Life's testings 30

Lord Jesus, you were tempted in all things as we are and you know the reality and power of such testings.

Have mercy on our human weakness, and give us strength in time of temptation to resist the evil one, in whatever guise he comes.

Help us to face all life's battles with courage and resolution, as good and faithful servants of the cross.

F.C.

From all blindness of heart,
from pride, vainglory, and hypocrisy,
from envy, hatred, and malice,
and from all uncharitableness,
    Good Lord, deliver us.

The Litany, Book of Common Prayer

A sense of humour 32

Lord, we know that life is not a joke. It is a serious and responsible business. But we also know that life has its lighter and amusing side.

So we thank you that among the many blessings you have given us is a sense of humour: the ability to laugh as well as to weep: to laugh with others and at others, and most of all to laugh at ourselves.

F.C.

Our future steps 33

Lord, since we know not what lies ahead of us in life's journey, guide our future steps in the way of your will; for in fulfilling your plan for our lives we shall be doing what is best for us, and most for your glory.

F.C.

WE ARE IN GOD'S HANDS

Providence 34

All as God wills, who wisely heeds
   To give or to withhold,
And knoweth more of all my needs
   Than all my prayers have told.

Thus more and more a providence
   Of love is understood,
Making the springs of time and sense
   Sweet with eternal good.

John Greenleaf Whittier (1802–92)

In God's hands 35

Lord, the Bible says, 'It is a fearful thing to fall into the hands of the living God.' So indeed it must be.

But surely, Lord, it would be a more fearful thing for us poor sinners to fall *out* of your hands: to be abandoned and left to our own devices in a world like ours.

Knowing well our weakness and helplessness, we

thankfully commit ourselves into your strong hands, assured that you will hold us fast all our days, and never let us go.

F.C.

Profit and loss   36

Teach us, dear Lord, frequently and attentively to consider this truth:
>   that if I gain the whole world and lose you, in the end I have lost everything;
>   whereas if I lose the world and gain you, in the end I have lost nothing.

John Henry Newman (1801–1890)

Life's changes   37

Dear Lord, through all the changing scenes of life keep my heart and mind open to the surprises of the Holy Spirit.

Give me your joy in accepting new ways, new thoughts, and new experiences, so that I may grow in grace to the end of my days.

Jean Coggan

My helper 38

'Where does my help come from?' asked the psalmist. And he answered, 'My help comes from the Lord'.
Yes, Lord, and my help comes from you too. Therefore I look to you for your help
   in my daily life and work,
   in times of need, illness, and anxiety,
   in facing my problems and difficulties.
So, come what may, I meet each day with serene faith and quietness of heart, *the Lord being my helper*.

F.C.

Journey's end 39

Come, Lord Jesus, come and possess our hearts.
Refresh us again with the vision of the holy city where you are worshipped and adored, the city we have longed for.
And at our journey's end welcome us home, to live with you for ever in the unfading glories of the courts of heaven.

Adapted

PART THREE

Everyday Life

HOME AND FAMILY

Our homes 40

Lord Jesus Christ, you lived in the home of Joseph and Mary at Nazareth: make our homes to be homes of love.

Deepen and sweeten every relationship of family life, so that all our earthly love may be gathered up into the love of God, for your name's sake.

*Harold Anson**

Family life 41

God our Father, you have commanded us to love one another and to serve each other's needs.

Help us in our homes to be helpful and considerate, forbearing and forgiving, so that the harmony of our family life may be strengthened and sustained.

So may the blessing of your peace rest upon us all, for Jesus Christ's sake.

Llewellyn Cumings

Heavenly Father, we thank you for our homes and families.

Make us aware of your loving care for us day by day and of all the blessings we receive which we take for granted; and help us to remember those who are lonely and less fortunate than ourselves, for our Saviour's sake.

Mothers' Union, Norwich Diocese

Our married partnership 43

Heavenly Father, send down upon us the dew of your heavenly grace in our married life, that we may have that joy in each other that passes not away; and having lived together in love here, may we ever live together in your glorious kingdom hereafter.

Bishop George Hicks (17th century)

Our children 44

God our Father, be near our children growing up in the perils and confusions of these times.

Guard them from the forces of evil at work in our society; lead them in the paths of goodness and truth; and enable us as parents to give them the security of our love, for our Saviour's sake.

F.C.

Lord Jesus, you watched the children at play; you took them in your arms and blessed them.

We pray for all children dear to us. Hold them in your arms of mercy and give them your blessing, that they may grow up in the knowledge of your love and give their lives to you, their Saviour and their Friend.

Llewellyn Cumings

Our food   46

Heavenly Father, we thank you for our daily meals, for the food which nourishes our bodies and strengthens our lives.

Make us grateful for all your good gifts to us, and deepen our trust in your love and care.

We ask it in Jesus' name.

F.C.

Our pets   47

O God, Lord of all creation, help us to treat with compassion the animals entrusted to our protection and care; and grant that in caring for them we may find a deeper understanding of your love for all creatures, great and small; through Christ our Lord.

Anon

WORK

Our daily work 48

Thank you, Lord for the gift of work and for the health and strength and brains which enable us to do it.

Help us to do our work well, and to work well with other people; and may we do our best to make the work of others easier and more pleasant; in the name of Jesus the carpenter, our Saviour.

*Christopher Idle**

49

God our Father, we thank you for calling us to be agents of your love in the world.

Help us to obey this calling in the place where we work, in our homes, and in our society; that we may be quick to seize opportunities of service, and wise to use them with loving care, for the honour of our Lord.

Basil Naylor

Those who work at home 50

We ask your blessing, our Father, on those whose
work lies in the privacy of their homes.

Give them patience, love, and a cheerful spirit, and
encourage them with the knowledge that in minister-
ing to those around them they are serving the Lord
Christ.

F.C.

Those who serve us 51

Lord God, you have bound us together in this bundle
of life: give us grace to understand how our lives de-
pend on the courage, industry and integrity of our
fellow-men; that we may be mindful of their needs,
grateful for their services, and faithful in our responsibilities to them.

Reinhold Niebuhr

The unemployed 52

God of all mercy, you made man in your image so that
he might find his joy and fulfilment in all that he does:
we pray that those in authority may so order our common life that all who are unemployed may have work
to do, and gain satisfaction in doing it; for Jesus
Christ's sake.

Anon

Bless, O Lord, all those who at the height of their powers have been deprived of their jobs. Help them and their families to adjust to this demand and deprivation, and enable them in their crisis to work together as a loving and courageous team; and grant that all who lose security of employment may find an inner security in Christ and in his service.

Dick Williams*

Money 54

Help us, good Lord, to understand the purpose and place of money in our life.

Keep before us the peril of loving it.

Help us to make it our servant, never our master.

And let neither the lack of it, nor the possession of it, in any degree loosen our grasp upon the heavenly riches, which are ours through the grace of Jesus Christ our Lord.

Dick Williams

55

Jesus, Lord and Master, make us faithful stewards of the money we earn, and of all that you have entrusted to us; that following your teaching we may learn to interpret life in terms of giving, not of getting, and be ready to use every opportunity of serving the needs of others, for the glory of your name.

F.C.

O God, give us work
   till our life shall end,
and give us life
   till our work is done.

Traditional

MORNING AND EVENING

At the beginning of the day 57

The day returns and brings us the petty round of irritating concerns and duties.

Help us, Lord, to perform them with laughter and kind faces. Let cheerfulness abound with industry.

Give us to go blithely on our business all this day; bring us to our resting beds weary and content and undishonoured; and grant us in the end the gift of sleep.

Robert Louis Stevenson (1850–1894)

58

All through this day, Lord Jesus, help me to be quick to praise, and slow to criticise, quick to forgive and slow to condemn, quick to share and slow to refuse to give.

So grant that I may help everyone and hurt no one, and find my true joy in living for others, not for myself.

Anon

Thank you, Lord, for a peaceful night's sleep and rest.

Now you have brought us to the beginning of a new day.

May it not be a wasted day, for it will never come again; so enable us to make full use of it and to spend it in ways that are pleasing to you and of help to others, for Christ's sake.

F.C.

60

Into your hands, O Lord, we commend ourselves and all who are dear to us.

Be with us in our going out and in our coming in; strengthen us for the work you have prepared for us to do; and grant that we may be so filled with your Holy Spirit that we may joyfully achieve all you want us to do; through Jesus Christ our Lord.

Bishop Theodore Woods

At this evening hour, O Lord, we come to you with thankful hearts to commit ourselves and those we love to your care and protection through the coming night.

Set free our minds from every anxiety and fear; and in your goodness and mercy grant us the gift of sleep to fit us for the duties and tasks of another day, through Christ our Lord.

F.C.

62

Be pleased, O merciful God, to protect us through the hours of this night, so that we who are wearied by the changes and chances of this life may rest in your eternal changelessness; through Jesus Christ our Lord.

The Office of Compline

63

Keep watch, O Lord, with those who work and watch and weep this night, and give your angels charge over those who sleep.

Tend the sick, Lord Christ, give rest to the weary, bless the dying, soothe the suffering, pity the afflicted, and all for your love's sake.

St Augustine (354–420)

PART FOUR

Our World

TODAY'S WORLD

What's wrong with the world? 64

Lord God, we live in a world where things have gone badly wrong because we have forgotten you and left you out of account.

We have worshipped other gods and have not hallowed your name.

We have adopted our own way of life and have not served your kingdom.

We have chosen what pleases us and have not done your will.

Lord, forgive our sin and folly and blindness, and turn us back to yourself, for the sake of your Son, the only Saviour of mankind.

F.C.

Lord, have mercy 65

Lord, have mercy on our wayward world, tottering on the brink of disaster and self-destruction.

Have mercy on the rulers and statesmen who bear the ultimate burden of government.

Have mercy on our own nation as we face our share of responsibility.

Lord, have mercy on us all, and grant us your salvation.

F.C.

God's world and ours 66

The world is yours, O God, for you created it and it belongs to you.

But the world is also ours, for you made it for our habitation.

Though 'the earth is the Lord's' and we do not own it, you have entrusted it to us your servants to care for and cultivate, to guard from waste and abuse; that in your goodness we may all enjoy the fruits of the earth, and with thankful hearts share them with all.

F.C.

Creation

Lord Christ, you have made us stewards and entrusted us with the wonders of your creation.

Instil within our minds a reverence for every living thing, lest in the hardness of our hearts we lose our reverence for life itself.

Frank Topping

Children of the world

Dear God, whose heart is as the heart of a child, hear our prayer for the children of the world, that they may grow in all that is honest, true and good.

Bless the disadvantaged, comfort the unloved, protect the neglected, give grace to the handicapped; and to all who care for children and nurture them, give patience, love, and faith, for Jesus' sake.

International Year of the Child

The world's pain 69

O Lord, so many sick, so many starving, so many deprived, so many sad, so many fearful:

when I look at them my heart fails;

when I look at you I hope again.

Help me to help you to reduce the world's pain,

O God of infinite compassion, O ceaseless energy of love.

George Appleton

World survey 70

We thank you, O Lord, that the future is bright, though the present is dark.

We pray for our world, especially for the nations where there is war and unrest.

We pray for those who suffer through poverty, malnutrition or disease.

We pray for those undergoing persecution through their faith and their stand for human rights.

May our efforts to help follow our prayers.

Come, Lord Jesus, to restore all to order and peace.

Jean Coggan

THE NATIONS OF THE WORLD

The nations 71

Look mercifully, O Lord our God, upon us and heal
the sorrows and sufferings of mankind.

Save the nations from the lust for power, from racial
hatred and jealousy, and from the worship of material
things.

Grant that in every land the rule of tyranny may be
broken and the cause of righteousness may triumph,
that people everywhere may learn to serve you in the
peace and freedom of your kingdom.

F.C.

The peace of the world 72

Lord God, we pray that your holy and life-giving
Spirit may so move in the hearts of men and among
the nations of the world that the barriers of fear, suspi-
cion and hatred which separate us may crumble, and
the body of mankind, being healed of its divisions,
may be united in the bonds of justice and peace, for
the honour of your name.

New Every Morning

Leaders of the nations 73

We pray, our Father, that when the interests and aspi-
rations of nations conflict with one another, their
leaders may not turn to war but together seek a just
and acceptable way forward, so that suspicions may
be allayed, misunderstandings clarified, violence aver-
ted, and peace preserved.
    We ask in the name of Christ our Lord.

Llewellyn Cumings

Peace in the Near East 74

Lord and creator of all the ends of the earth, we pray
for peace among the children of Abraham.
    Where Jew and Moslem and Christian are op-
pressed by their history and their hatred, restrain the
wicked and strengthen the peace-makers.
    Make us aware, beyond our despair, of your aching
heart of love for all peoples, our one God and one judge.

John Poulton

The Jews 75

O God, the God of Abraham, remember your everlasting covenant, and bring back your chosen people to
your love and truth; that as they know you to be the
only God, they may acknowledge Jesus, whom you
have sent to be our Messiah and Saviour.

David Silk

Racial harmony

God our Father, who made of one blood all nations to dwell upon the earth, deepen our understanding of peoples of other races, languages and customs.

Teach us to view them in the light of your own all-embracing love; and give us a vision of the true brotherhood of mankind, united under one Father, in the faith of the one Lord, our Saviour Jesus Christ.

Adapted

Nuclear power

Almighty God, without whom all things hasten to destruction and fall into nothingness, look mercifully upon your family of nations, to which you have committed power in trust for their mutual health and comfort.

Save us and help us, O Lord, lest we abuse your gift and make it our misery and ruin; and renew our faith in your unchanging purpose of goodwill and peace on earth, for the love of Jesus Christ our Lord.

Frederick Macnutt

OUR OWN NATION

Our nation   78

God bless our land;
God guide our rulers;
God revive our churches;
God resolve our differences;
God protect our homes;
God strengthen our faith;
   for the sake of Christ our Lord.

Maurice Wood

79

God of our fathers, as we thank you for your mercy
towards our nation throughout its long history, we
seek your continuing mercy in this our day.

Deliver us from the sins of affluence, from pride,
from materialism, and from indifference to the needs
of the world.

Give to our leaders soundness of judgement in making their decisions; and unite us all in a common zeal
to honour you and serve mankind; through Christ our
Lord.

John R.W. Stott

Those in authority 80

Heavenly Father, we pray for our Queen and for all those under her who guide and govern our national life.

Fill them with the fear of your holy name, that they may be set free from the fear of man.

Help them in every situation to know and do the thing that is right and good, and overrule all their deliberations for the welfare of our people and for your own glory.

F.C.

Social justice 81

Holy Spirit of light and truth, help us to understand the causes of our social tensions and unrest.

Open our eyes to economic wrongs and injustices; deepen our concern for the old, the poor, and the handicapped; and stir in us all a burning sense of responsibility for one another, as servants of Jesus Christ our Lord.

Basil Naylor

Recall to religion

Almighty God, to forget whom is to stumble and fall,
to remember whom is to rise again: mercifully draw
the people of this country to yourself.

Prosper all efforts to make known to them the truth
of the gospel, that many may learn their need of you
and your love for them; that so your Church and kingdom may be established to the glory of your name;
through Jesus Christ our Lord.

A national prayer, 1937

Northern Ireland

Father, we pray for Northern Ireland, its politicians
and people. Give them the will to seek reconciliation
and justice, and to find stable government and peace.

Grant that as the Holy Spirit worked at the first,
breaking down the dividing wall between Jew and
Gentile, and creating one new humanity in Christ, so
by the same Spirit Protestants and Catholics may find
in Christ the freedom to live together and care for one
another in his name.

Adapted

THE WORLD'S AFFLICTED PEOPLE

The destitute 84

Make us worthy, Lord, to serve our fellow-men throughout the world who live and die in poverty and hunger.

Give them, through our hands, this day their daily bread, and by our understanding love give peace and joy.

Mother Teresa of Calcutta

Refugees 85

Lord Jesus Christ, who in perfect love for mankind chose to live as one who had nowhere to lay his head, we pray for refugees in today's world: all who must live in exile or in a strange land for their home.

Grant them human help and friendship in their need, the chance of a new beginning, and courage to take it; and above all an abiding faith in your love and care; for your name's sake.

Christian Aid*

The persecuted 86

Lord God, the refuge and strength of your people in every time of need, we pray for those who are persecuted for their religious faith or their political opinions.

Give them strength to endure their afflictions, grace to forgive their persecutors, and courage to maintain their testimony until the day of their deliverance.

James Todd

The hungry 87

God our Father, in the name of him who gave bread to the hungry, we remember all who through our human ignorance, selfishness and folly are condemned to live in want; and we pray that all endeavours for the overcoming of world hunger and poverty may be so prospered that there may be food sufficient for all.

*Christian Aid**

Children in need 88

Heavenly Father, we commend to your compassion all homeless children and orphans, and all whose lives are overshadowed by cruelty and violence, or thwarted by disease.

Awaken in us all your living charity, and bless those who work for the welfare of children in any kind of need, for Christ our Saviour's sake.

New Every Morning

PART FIVE

The Church

MEMBERSHIP AND FELLOWSHIP

Our baptism 89

God our Father, in our baptism you welcomed us into the family of your Church, and made us one with Christ in his death and resurrection.

Help us to remember what this means to us personally; that we who have been signed with the sign of the cross may never be ashamed to confess the faith of Christ crucified, and acknowledge him as our risen Saviour and Lord, to the honour of his name.

F.C.

Our church 90

We thank you, Lord, for the church of which we are members, and pray your blessing on all who share with us in its life and worship.

Save us as a congregation from being inward looking, over-occupied with our own little affairs. Help us to take our eyes off ourselves and turn them on those outside, always remembering that the Church of Christ exists not for itself but for the sake of others and to spread abroad far and wide the good news of his great salvation.

F.C.

Lord God, give grace to your Church,
 here and in every place,
to offer a living worship to you
 in your majesty and glory,
and a living witness to the world
 in its need of your salvation.

F.C.

Church fellowship 92

Lord Jesus, you have redeemed us and called us to share in the life of your Church.

We thank you for our fellow-Christians, travellers with us on the way of life, who worship and work with us in the life of our church.

Bind us together in your service, and always keep us close to you as well as to one another, for your name's sake.

Llewellyn Cumings

93

We praise you, O God, for the fellowship of the Spirit, who unites us in the bond of peace as members of the one Body.

Deepen our communion one with another in Christ, and grant that through your Spirit continually working in us we may increase in the knowledge of your love, and learn to love our Christian brothers and sisters with the love you have shown to us in Jesus Christ our Lord.

Anon

CHURCH WORSHIP

True worship 94

Our Father, help us to worship you in the Spirit, with our minds nourished by your truth, our hearts opened to your love, our wills surrendered to your purpose; and may all this be gathered up in adoration as we ascribe glory and praise to you alone; through Jesus Christ our Lord.

William Temple*

For acceptable worship 95

Almighty God, who pours out on all who desire it the spirit of praise and adoration; deliver us, when we draw near to you, from coldness of heart and wandering of mind; that with steadfast thoughts and kindled affections we may worship you in spirit and in truth; through Jesus Christ our Lord.

William Bright

Father, as we turn aside from the busy world,
    with its clamour and distractions,
quieten our hearts in your presence,
    that we may be still
    and know that you are God,
our God, now and for ever, through Christ our Lord.

                                                            F.C.

Joy in worship 97

Father, may we be glad when it is said to us, 'Let us go
to the house of the Lord!'

    May it be our delight as well as our duty to worship
you in the fellowship of the Church.

    Prepare us in mind and spirit as we go to the house
of the Lord, and let our hearts be tuned to sing your
praise and make a joyful noise to the Lord.

    So may we with heart and voice glorify your holy
name, through Christ our Saviour.

                                                            F.C.

United worship   98

Eternal God and Father, unite us as we worship you
with all who in far-off places are lifting up their hands
and hearts to you; that your Church throughout the
world, with the Church in heaven, may offer up one
sacrifice of praise and thanksgiving, to your honour
and glory.

Anon

Holy Communion   99

Lord, this is your feast,
    spread at your command,
    attended at your invitation,
    blessed by your own word,
    distributed by your own hand,
    the undying memorial of your sacrifice,
    the full gift of your everlasting love.
So may we come, O Lord, to your table;
    Lord Jesus, come to us.

Eric Milner-White

100

Come to us, Lord Jesus, and preside as host at your
table in the sacrament of our redemption.

May it be to us not only a memorial of your saving
passion but a means of grace to our souls, and a pledge
of our eternal inheritance, your heavenly banquet; that
renewed in spirit we may live more truly as your disciples in the world, to the honour of your name.

F.C.

O Lamb of God, Saviour of the world, be to us at every eucharist the heavenly Bread, the true Vine; that we may feed on your body and blood by faith, lifting up our hearts in thanksgiving, and presenting ourselves to you a living sacrifice to your glory.

F.C.

Preparation for Communion 102

Most gracious Father, you invite us to the holy table of our Saviour to show his death and receive his gift of eternal life: enable us to come with earnest faith and kindled devotion.

Help us to make the memorial of our Saviour's sacrifice with adoration and praise; and grant that, yielding ourselves to you, we may henceforth live as those who are not their own but bought with a price, through the love of Jesus Christ our Lord.

From the Church of Scotland liturgy

Lord Jesus, your table is spread, and we come as your guests to partake of these tokens of your love and passion, your body broken for us, your blood shed for us.

We are not worthy to receive you; but come to us and dwell with us, and deepen our love for you, our faith in you, our communion with you; and fill our hearts with the joy of your salvation.

F.C.

104

Come, Lord Jesus, in the fullness of your grace
    and dwell in the hearts of us your servants;
that adoring you by faith
    we may with joy receive you,
and with love and thankfulness abide in you.
    our Guide, our Bread of pilgrims,
    our Comrade by the way.

E.D. Sedding, SSJE

CHURCH UNITY

One Body   105

God and Father of us all, though as Christians we
belong to various communions, we thank you for the
unity which is already ours as members of the one
Body of Christ.

We pray that this spiritual unity may, by your grace,
increasingly become a visible unity, so that the Church
in every place may demonstrate the reconciling power
of the gospel, and the reality of your love for all mankind, in Christ your Son.

F.C.

A fellowship of the Spirit   106

God our Father, bless your Church with unity, peace
and concord. Make it here and all over the world a
true fellowship of the Spirit in which no distinction is
made because of colour, class or party; a fellowship of
love in which all are really one in Christ.

We ask it in his name, who is our one Lord.

William Barclay

Lord and heavenly Father,
through your Son Jesus Christ
you have called us to be one
in the family of your Church:
give us grace to break down the barriers
which keep us apart;
that accepting our differences,
we may grow in love for one another,
to the glory of your name.

A prayer from Northern Ireland

Unity and peace 108

Lord Jesus Christ, you said to your apostles, 'I leave
you peace, my peace I give you': look not on our sins
but on the faith of your Church, and grant us the peace
and unity of your kingdom, where you live for ever
and ever.

Roman Catholic Order of Mass

Father, we pray for your Church throughout the world, that it may share to the full in the work of your Son, revealing you to men and reconciling men to you and to one another; that we and all Christian people may learn to love one another as you have loved us, and your Church may more and more reflect the unity which is your will and your gift, in Jesus Christ our Lord.

Chapel of Unity, Coventry Cathedral

THE CHURCH'S MISSION

Evangelism 110

Father, you have committed to us the good news of your saving love, and set us as ambassadors for Christ in your world.

Help us together to bear witness to the message of reconciliation, that in the life of your Church men and women may become new creatures in Jesus Christ our Lord.

Collects with the New Lectionary

Good news 111

Lord Jesus, when we hear good news we are eager to share it with others.

As Christians we have all heard the gospel, with its good news of the forgiveness of sins and the gift of eternal life through your cross and resurrection.

May we not keep this good news to ourselves. May we share it with those around us, not by preaching to them but by testifying in a simple way to what you have done for us, and mean to us, as our living Saviour and Lord.

F.C.

Lord Christ, your last word to your disciples before you left this earth was that they should preach the gospel in all the world and to every nation.

We thank you for all who since then have obeyed your command, and for those who brought the gospel to our own shores; and we ask you to show us how to make the good news meaningful to our own generation and in our own community, for the honour and praise of your name.

F.C.

113

Lord, in your mercy rekindle the faith and love of your people in every place.

Fill them with an urgent desire to spread the gospel near and far, that all may hear the good news of your redeeming love, and know for themselves that you died for them, and that you are the Saviour of the world, and their Saviour too.

Adapted

Renewal of the Church 114

Lord God, in Christ you make all things new.
    Grant to your Church a new vision of your glory,
    a new experience of your power,
    a new consecration to your service;
that through the witness of a renewed and dedicated
people your work may be revived and your kingdom
extended among us, for the honour of your name.

F.C.

The caring Church 115

Most merciful Father, you have called us to be a caring
Church, reflecting in our lives your infinite care for us
your children.
    Help us to fulfil our calling and to care for one an-
other in an unselfish fellowship of love; and to care for
the world around us by sharing with it the good news
of your love, and serving those who suffer from poverty, hunger and disease; in the name of Christ our
Lord.

Based on words of Michael Ramsey

PART SIX

Christian Faith and Life

CHRISTIAN FAITH AND LIFE

Personal faith   116

> My faith looks up to thee,
> Thou Lamb of Calvary,
>   Saviour divine;
> Now hear me while I pray,
> Take all my guilt away,
> O let me from this day
>   Be wholly thine.

Ray Palmer (1808–1887)

Faith's object   117

Lord, we do not ask for great faith but for faith in a great Saviour.

We have come to see that the efficacy of our faith depends not on its size but on its object. And we know full well the true object of our faith.

Therefore we pray that we may run the race before us with our eyes fixed on *Jesus*, on whom faith depends from start to finish: Jesus, who endured the shameful cross and is now seated at the right hand of the throne of God.

Based on Hebrews 12. 1,2

Forgiveness of sins

Forgive me my sins, O Lord: the sins of my present and the sins of my past, the sins of my soul and the sins of my body. Forgive my casual sins and my deliberate sins, and those which I have laboured so long to hide that I have hidden them even from myself.

Forgive me them, O Lord, forgive them all, for the sake of Jesus Christ my Saviour.

Bishop Thomas Wilson (1663–1755)

For compassion

Father, help us, who through your mercy have been forgiven, to be compassionate to those who have fallen into sin, considering how we ourselves have fallen in times past; and may we neither presume on your forgiveness by living carelessly, nor doubt it by being weighed down by guilt; for Jesus Christ's sake.

Adapted

For humility 120

Lord Jesus, on the night before your passion you met
with your disciples, and taking towel and water you
stooped and washed their feet.

Give us understanding of what you did then, and
teach us to follow the example of your humility, that
with love we may serve one another, for your sake.

F.C.

The incarnate Christ 121

Eternal Lord Christ, in your great humility you were
born of the Virgin Mary and became the Son of Man,
that we might become the sons of God.

We pray that as you came to share in our humanity,
so we may share the life of your divinity, and reflect
your image in all we are and do.

Adapted

The living Christ

The Lord is risen! and we are risen with him.
The Lord is risen! and life eternal is ours.
The Lord is risen! and death has lost its sting.
The Lord is risen! and the way to heaven is open.
The Lord is risen! he is risen indeed.
Alleluia!

F.C.

Holy Spirit

Holy Spirit of God,
Spirit of grace and life,
breathe into us your love,
your joy, your peace;
that quickened by your power
our lives may be renewed in Christ
after his likeness.

Michael Perry *

124

Lord Jesus, may the fire of your Holy Spirit
consume in us all that displeases you,
and kindle in our hearts a burning zeal
for the service of your kingdom;
through our Saviour Jesus Christ.

From an ancient collect

Discrimination

Lord, in the world around us our lives are inevitably influenced for good or evil by books and newspapers, radio and television.

Teach us to discriminate in the things we read and hear and see: to spurn the false, the superficial, the degrading, and to choose whatever things are true and honourable, just and pure, as befits those who honour the name of Jesus Christ our Lord.

F.C.

Supersitition: a false faith

Good Lord, deliver us from the snare of superstition: from a false faith, from foolish and irrational beliefs.

Our lives are not ruled by chance, nor are they dependent on luck or the stars or any such fantasies.

You are our God. You are on the throne. Our times are in your hands. *The Lord reigns!* Let that be our confidence and our comfort, and let our faith be wholly centred on your Son Jesus Christ, who alone is the Way, the Truth and the Life.

F.C.

God's loving wisdom 127

What is before us in life we know not; but this we know, that all things are ordered with unerring wisdom and unbounded love by you, our God. Grant us in all things to see your hand; through Jesus Christ our Lord.

*Charles Simeon (1759–1836)**

The kingdom of God 128

Yours, Lord, is the kingdom, yours the sovereign rule that changes life and makes all things new.

May your kingship be acknowledged in all the world, that the reign of sin may be broken, and the people of every nation learn to live in freedom and peace, through Christ our Lord.

F.C.

The spiritual war 129

Lord God, you have called us to be soldiers of Jesus Christ and to fight manfully under his banner.

Enable us at all times to contend for justice, truth and goodness, and relentlessly to oppose evil, wherever it is found and whatever form it takes, for the honour of your name.

F.C.

Reverence for life 130

Eternal Father, source of life and light, whose love extends to all creatures, all things: grant us that reverence for life which becomes those who believe in you, lest we despise it or come callously to destroy it.

Rather let us save it, secure it, and sanctify it, after the example of your Son, Jesus Christ our Lord.

Robert Runcie

The life to come 131

Eternal God and Father, give us grace to believe that what was created in love and redeemed by love has in love's design a future and fulfilment worthy of that love.

Therefore in the faith of him who said, 'I am the resurrection and the life', we entrust to you our dear ones and ourselves, as to a faithful Creator and most merciful Saviour; through our Lord Jesus Christ.

*Father Andrew**

PART SEVEN

Prayers of Christian Devotion

OUR LORD JESUS CHRIST

King of glory   132

You are the King of glory, O Christ,
   the eternal Son of the Father.
When you became man to redeem mankind
   you did not shun the Virgin's womb.
When you overcame the sting of death
   you opened the kingdom of heaven to all believers.
You are seated at the right hand of God
   in the glory of the Father.

Te Deum Laudamus

To whom shall we go?   133

Lord, to whom shall we go?
You have the words of eternal life.
   I believe in you.
   I love you.
   I trust you.
   I give myself to you.
   Give yourself to me.
Come, Lord Jesus, come quickly.

Archbishop Goodier

My heart

Lord Jesus, my heart is cold:
    warm it with your selfless love.
My heart is sinful:
    cleanse it by your precious blood.
My heart is empty:
    fill it with your divine presence.
Lord Jesus, my heart is yours:
    possess it always and only for yourself.

Maurice Wood

The hungry soul

Jesu, thou joy of loving hearts,
    Thou fount of life, thou light of men;
From the best bliss that earth imparts,
    We turn unfilled to thee again.

We taste thee, O thou living Bread,
    And long to feast upon thee still;
We drink of thee, the fountain head,
    And thirst our souls from thee to fill.

Ray Palmer (1808–1887)

Praise to our Redeemer 136

To him who loves us,
and has freed us from our sins by his blood,
and has made us a kingdom and priests
  to serve his God and Father,
to him be glory and power
  for ever and ever!

Revelation 1. 5,6

Wonderful Saviour 137

We praise you, Lord Jesus, for you are wonderful:
  wonderful in the words you spoke,
  wonderful in the works you wrought,
  wonderful in the death you suffered,
  wonderful in the triumph you won,
  wonderful in your love for sinners.
    Glory to your name.

F.C.

Blessed Jesus, you are always near
   in times of stress.
Though we cannot feel your presence
   you are close.
You are always there
   to help and watch over us.
Nothing in heaven or on earth
   can part you from us.

Derived from Margery Kempe (15th century)

The Way, the Truth, and the Life 139

Lord Jesus Christ, you declared yourself to be the Way, the Truth, and the Life.

Help us not to stray from you, for you are the Way; nor to distrust you, for you are the Truth; nor to rest on any other than you, for you are the Life.

Give us grace to follow you, the Way, to learn from you, the Truth, and live in you, the Life.

After Erasmus (16th century)

Invocation

Come, our Light, and illumine our darkness.
Come, our Life, and raise us from death.
Come, our Physician, and heal our wounds.
Come, Flame of divine Love, and burn up our sins.
Come, our King, sit upon the throne of our hearts and
  reign there.

St Dimitrii of Rostov (17th century)

Commitment to Christ

Lord Christ, we are not our own, for you have redeemed us by your precious blood: we thankfully
commit our lives to you.

Take us as we are, and make us what you want us to
be; and so strengthen us by your Holy Spirit that we
may give ourselves to your service, to the glory of God
the Father.

F.C.

OTHER PRAYERS

God is love 142

Holy and Blessed Trinity, Father, Son, and Holy Spirit, you are love, and from you flows that love which is the source of all love.

Your love draws us together, as members of your family, in a deep and eternal unity.

Your love calls from us the response of our own love, and the adoration we give you in worship, to the honour and glory of your name.

Christ Church, Fulwood

Love for God 143

O God, who hast prepared for them that love thee such good things as pass man's understanding: pour into our hearts such love toward thee, that we, loving thee above all things, may obtain thy promises, which exceed all that we can desire; through Jesus Christ our Lord.

Book of Common Prayer

A forgiving spirit 144

O Lord, because we so often sin and ask for pardon,
help us to forgive as we have been forgiven; neither
mentioning old offences committed against us, nor
dwelling upon them in thought, nor being influenced
by them in heart, but loving our brother freely, as thou
freely lovest us; for Christ's sake.

Christina Rossetti (1830–1894)

The heart of a child 145

Grant me, O God, the heart of a child,
    pure and transparent as a stream;
a simple heart, glorious in self-giving,
    tender in compassion;
a heart faithful and generous;
    which will never forget any good
    or bear a grudge for any evil.
Grant me, O God, the mind and heart
    of your dear Son.

George Appleton

Belonging

I thank you, O God, that I am not a lonely, solitary, isolated being.

I belong to you, for you are my Father, and you belong to me, for I am your child.

I belong! Lord, what an unspeakable mercy that is; for

> *I nothing lack if I am his*
> *and he is mine for ever.*

F.C.

Christ's bondslave

> Make me a captive, Lord,
>   and then I shall be free;
> Force me to render up my sword,
>   and I shall conqueror be.
> I sink in life's alarms
>   when by myself I stand;
> Imprison me within thine arms,
>   and strong shall be my hand.

George Matheson (1842–1906)

The gift of peace 148

Lord God, you are peace eternal, and your chosen reward is the gift of peace.

Pour your peace into our souls, that everything discordant may utterly vanish, and all that makes for peace be loved and sought by us always; through Christ our Saviour.

From an ancient Latin prayer

Dedication 149

Here I am, Lord, body, heart and soul.
Grant that, with your love,
I may be big enough to reach the world,
and small enough to be at one with you.

Mother Teresa of Calcutta

The judgement-seat of Christ 150

Lord Jesus Christ, before whose judgement-seat we all must appear and give account of the things done in the body, grant that when the books are opened in that day, the faces of your servants may not be ashamed; through your merits, O blessed Saviour, who lives and reigns with the Father and the Holy Spirit, one God, world without end.

Episcopal Church of Scotland

PART EIGHT

Sectional Prayers

PRAYERS IN THE CELTIC TRADITION
from various sources, Gaelic in origin

The homestead 151

God bless the world and all that is therein,
God bless my spouse and my children,
God bless the eye that is within my head,
God bless the handling of my hand,
   what time I rise in the morning early,
   what time I lie down late in bed.

God guide me 152

God guide me with thy wisdom,
God help me with thy mercy,
God protect me with thy strength,
God fill me with thy grace,
for the sake of thine anointed Son.

May the right hand of the Lord
  keep us ever in old age;
May the grace of Christ
  continually defend us from the enemy.
O Lord, direct our hearts in the way of peace,
  through Jesus Christ our Lord.

Joy   154

As the hand is made for holding and the eye for
seeing, thou hast fashioned me for joy, O God.
  Share with me in finding that joy everywhere: in the
violet's beauty, in the lark's melody, in the child's face,
in a mother's love, in the purity of Jesus.

Peace   155

Lord, thou didst command peace:
  thou gavest peace.
Thou didst bequeath peace;
  give us thy peace from heaven.
Make this day peaceful,
  and the remaining days of our life.

Holding God's hand 156

Lord, as the rain hides the stars, as the clouds veil the blue sky, so the dark happenings of my lot hide the shining of thy face from me.

Yet if I may hold thy hand in the darkness, it is enough, since I know that, though I may stumble in my going, thou dost not fall.

Morning prayer 157

Thanks be to thee, Jesus Christ,
who brought'st me up from last night
to the gladsome light of this day,
to win everlasting life for my soul,
through the blood thou didst shed for me.
    Praise be to thee, O Lord, for ever.

Benedictions 158

May the road rise to meet you,
may the wind be always at your back,
may the sun shine warm upon your face,
may the rain fall softly on your field,
may God hold you in the hollow of his hand.

Deep peace of the running wave to you,
Deep peace of the flowing air to you,
Deep peace of the quiet earth to you,
Deep peace of the shining stars to you,
Deep peace of the Son of Peace to you.

Iona Community

TRANSATLANTIC PRAYERS
of the Episcopal Church
of the USA

For the Human Family 160

O God, you made us in your own image and redeemed us through Jesus Christ your Son: look with
compassion on the whole human family.

Take away the arrogance and hatred which infect
our hearts; break down the walls that separate us;
unite us in bonds of love; and work through our strug-
gle and confusion to accomplish your purposes on
earth; through Jesus Christ our Lord.

For young persons 161

God our Father, you see our children growing up in an
unsteady and confusing world: show them that your
ways give more life than the ways of the world, and
that following you is better than chasing after selfish
goals. Give them strength to hold their faith in you,
and to keep alive their joy in your creation; through
Jesus Christ our Lord.

For the good use of leisure 162

O God, in the course of this busy life, give us times of refreshment and peace; and grant that we may so use our leisure to rebuild our bodies and renew our minds that our spirits may be opened to the goodness of your creation; through Jesus Christ our Lord.

For the right use of God's gifts 163

Almighty God, whose loving hand has given us all that we possess: grant us grace that we may honour you with our substance; and remembering the account which we must one day give, may be faithful stewards of your bounty; through Jesus Christ our Lord.

For social justice 164

Grant, O God, that your holy and life-giving Spirit may so move the hearts of the people of this land, that barriers which divide us may crumble, suspicions disappear, and hatreds cease; that our divisions being healed, we may live in justice and peace; through Jesus Christ our Lord.

In times of conflict 165

O God, you have bound us together in a common life.
Help us, in the midst of our struggles for justice and
truth, to confront one another without hatred or bitter-
ness, and to work together with mutual forbearance
and respect; through Jesus Christ our Lord.

For the future of the human race 166

O God our heavenly Father, you have blessed us and
given us dominion over all the earth: increase our reverence before the mystery of life; and give us new
insight into your purposes for the human race, and
new wisdom and determination in making provision
for its future in accordance with your will; through
Jesus Christ our Lord.

For a quiet mind 167

O God of peace, you have taught us that in returning
and rest we shall be saved, in quietness and in confidence shall be our strength: by the might of your Spirit
lift us, we pray, to your presence, where we may be
still and know that you are God; through Jesus Christ
our Lord.

A MEDLEY OF SHORT PRAYERS

The mind of Christ 168

Holy Spirit of God, bring my mind into harmony with the mind of Christ, that I may think and say and do all things to his glory.

F.C.

God's love 169

Father, seeing how freely you have loved me with my inperfections, grant that I may equally love others with theirs.

Anon

Nearness to God 170

Be not far from us, O God, and in your mercy guide our footsteps that we wander not from you, for Jesus Christ's sake.

Grace and gratitude 171

Father, give me your grace when things go wrong, and when things go right make me grateful.

F.C.

Perils of abundance 172

Lord, mercifully grant that we may not become so occupied with material things, that having gained the whole world we lose our soul.

G.W. Briggs

Our greatest need 173

O Lord, never suffer us to think we can stand by ourselves and not need thee, who art our greatest need.

John Donne (1571–1631)

Enlightenment 174

Lord, may your Spirit so enlighten our minds that we may have a better understanding of your truth and a clearer vision of your love.

F.C.

Commitment   175

O Lord Jesus Christ, who hast brought me where I am
upon my way: thou knowest what thou wouldest do
with me; do with me according to thy will.

King Henry VI (1421–1471)

Life's direction   176

O Lord, make thy way plain before me. Let thy glory
be my end, thy Word my rule, and then thy will be
done.

King Charles I (1600–1649)

A bedtime prayer   177

I will lie down in peace and take my rest; for it is you,
Lord, only who makes me dwell in safety.

From the Office of Compline (Psalm 4.8)

A fourfold prayer 178

O Lord, heal our infirmities, pardon our offences, lighten our burdens, enrich our poverty; through Christ our Lord.

Christopher Sutton (16th century)

Life's small duties 179

Father, light up the small duties of this day's life. May they shine with the beauty of thy countenance, and may we believe that glory dwells in the commonest tasks.

J.H. Jowett

Worship and witness 180

Grant, O Lord, that we who worship thee in thy church may be witnesses to thee in thy world.

A. Campbell Fraser

Acknowledgements

Grateful acknowledgement is made to the following for prayers reproduced in this book.

Hodder and Stoughton for prayers from *Contemporary Parish Prayers* (nos. 21, 55, 109) and *New Parish Prayers* (nos. 44, 66, 67, 71, 74, 79, 97, 118), both edited by Frank Colquhoun.

BBC Publications for prayers from *New Every Morning*, 1973, edited by Frank Colquhoun.

The Episcopal Church of the United States of America for prayers from the Book of Common Prayer 1977.

Lady Coggan, the Revd Llewellyn Cumings, Bishop Richard Harries, Cardinal Basil Hume, the Revd Christopher Idle, the Revd Michael Perry, Lord Runcie, Archdeacon David Silk, the Revd John Stott, the Revd Dick Williams, Bishop Maurice Wood.

Extracts from *The Book of Common Prayer* (1662), the rights of which are vested in the Crown in perpetuity within the United Kingdom, are reproduced by permission of Cambridge University Press, Her Majesty's Printers.

Index of Principal Subjects